TACOMA, WASHINGTON. *See page iv.*

TROLLEYS AND STREETCARS
ON AMERICAN PICTURE POSTCARDS

by
Ray D. Appelgate

Dover Publications, Inc.
New York

ACKNOWLEDGMENTS

In putting together this book of trolley postcards, I have received a great deal of information and encouragement from Felix Reifschneider of Fairton, N.J., who for years has written and published many books on trolleys.

O. R. Cummings of Manchester, N.H., one of the most prolific writers on trolley history in America, gave me much detailed information on the publication of the cards.

Louis W. Goodwin of Northfield, Conn., a great collector of trolley and railroad memorabilia, read my manuscript and made many valuable suggestions.

From the postcard angle, Richard T. Donovan of Hollywood, Florida, spent much time selecting those cards in my collection with the greatest eye appeal and interest.

For specific information on certain cards, I want to thank: Roger Arcara (Bronx, N.Y.), George Basch (Jamaica, N.Y.), Russell Bennett (Pittsfield, Mass.), Wray Brown (Yakima, Wash.), James Browning (Beaverton, Ore.), Peter S. Charow (Greenfield, Mass.), Frank Drew (Klamath Falls, Ore.), James Drummond (Westfield, Mass.), James R. Eaton (West Springfield, Mass.), Robert B. Eaton (Kent, Wash.), Bruce D. Elfreth (Stuart, Fla.), Allan H. MacDougall (Milan, N.H.), William Nedden (Milwaukee, Wis.), Ronald M. Peck (Canaan, N.Y.), Edward Ridolph (Lake Worth, Fla.), Duane F. Sumner (Bancroft, Mich.), Richard H. Steinmetz (Camp Hill, Pa.), Mrs. Marie Tassone (Great Barrington, Mass.) and James D. White (New York, N.Y.).

Frontispiece: TACOMA, WASHINGTON. Tacoma Municipal Railway. This peculiarly shaped car, its back end of a different design from the front, is following a two-car train of an interurban line. The Tacoma Municipal Railway (7 miles, 38 cars) was owned by the city but was operated by the Tacoma Railway and Power Co. under a profit-sharing arrangement. (Original-photograph card; n.d.)

Published in Canada by General Publishing Company, Ltd., 30 Lesmill Road, Don Mills, Toronto, Ontario.
Published in the United Kingdom by Constable and Company, Ltd., 10 Orange Street, London WC2H 7EG.

Trolleys and Streetcars on American Picture Postcards is a new work, first published by Dover Publications, Inc., in 1979.

International Standard Book Number: 0-486-23749-4
Library of Congress Catalog Card Number: 78-64854

Manufactured in the United States of America
Dover Publications, Inc.
180 Varick Street
New York, N.Y. 10014

INTRODUCTION

Interestingly enough, the heyday of trolleys and the postcard craze paralleled each other very closely. The picture postcard did not come into common use in the United States until after the turn of the century. In earlier examples, pictures had generally been printed on the back of government-issued penny postcards, such as those with views of the Columbian Exposition in Chicago in 1893. But the postcards did not really get under way until the government approved private manufacture of cards in 1898, and even then they took several years to catch on.

It was about 1902 that the postcard craze hit the country, lasting right up to our entry into World War I in the spring of 1917. Collectors would send postcards to total strangers in faraway places, asking for local cards in return. Some collectors specialized in courthouses, churches, Y.M.C.A.'s, railroad depots, prisons, county poor farms, old ladies' homes, Masonic temples, even cemeteries; others collected anything they could find. Postcard albums, bought by the millions, were filled with every sort of postcard ever issued. The craze was actually worldwide, since many countries had postcards, and a great deal of geography was learned in the course of international exchanges.

The Post Office was a very different organization in the early part of the century, far more efficient and faster than it is today. The postcard craze doubled and tripled its business, and many changes were made to accommodate it. Before March 1, 1907, it was illegal to write any message on the same side of the card as the address. For that reason the early postcards have handwriting all over the sides of the picture, and sometimes right across it. Many an otherwise beautiful card was defaced in this way. There is some occasional handwriting on items in this book, but this is easy to overlook and forgive in the case of very fine cards. Not only was the message restriction removed because of the craze, but other encumbrances were done away with. When postcards first started to go through the mails, they were postmarked at the receiving post of-fice as well as that of the sender, making it easy to see the time involved between post offices—sometimes remarkably brief! The volume of postcards was an important reason for discontinuing the unnecessary second marking about 1910.

Not only was the entire railroad system geared to transporting the mails from town to town, but interurban and even local trolleys participated. Many cars had a mail slot on the side or end, and the mail receptacle was emptied each time they passed the post office. And all for a penny a card postage, right up to World War II. For years the postcards themselves cost only a nickel for six.

The postcards consisting of a real photograph were the finest in accuracy, but probably the most popular American postcards up to the First World War were those made in Germany from photographs supplied by American publishers. At the time of the postcard craze, of course, color photography was still something of a rarity and not commercially viable. For the color cards, black-and-white photos were touched up, hand-colored with tracing paper, and then generally reproduced by lithography. The pictures were transferred to the lithographic stone, offset onto a rubber blanket and printed from that onto paper.

Since the German artists had never visited the scenes they were coloring, they could often only guess the colors of the trolleys, buildings and other elements of the views, unless the American publisher told them what colors to use. The details in the German cards, however, were extremely sharp, and the best of them technically have never been matched since. Postcard manufacturing became a big business in Germany, where it was said there were more postcard shops than groceries. The Austrians, who were the first ever to use postcards, in 1869, were producing also. The British had some very good cards, especially those by Raphael Tuck. Among the best manufactured here in the United States were the ''Phostint'' cards of the Detroit Publishing Company and those of Edward H. Mitchell in San Francisco.

The German postcard industry folded up like an accordion in the summer of 1914, when the war struck Europe, and never revived. Three years later, the United States entered the war, and the postcard craze ended.

Trolleys preceded postcards in America by just a few years. In Richmond, Virginia in 1888, Frank Sprague, the inventor of the first successful trolley car to run by electricity, managed to get 22 trolleys up a hill at the same time, on the same track and each on its own power. From that time on, the horsecar was steadily and rapidly replaced by the electric car. Everywhere new lines spread out like spiderwebs from "central city," as the downtown transfer point was called, to the suburbs; in fact, building the trolley line became the first act in establishing new developments. Every city, and most small towns, had a "Toonerville Trolley" to meet all the trains. As soon as the local trolleys were firmly established, interurbans started to connect cities and towns, and even began to threaten the railroad's domination of the transportation industry. Trolleys also went into the baggage and freight business, often seriously competing with the railroads.

Trolley development reached its peak about 1918 and then, very slowly at first, but later more rapidly, the companies went into bankruptcy and the cars disappeared from the American scene. Trolley lines were bought and sold and big conglomerates were formed, but in the end the automobile drove out the trolley.

The postcard craze was in full swing during the formative years of the trolley lines, and the cars were an extremely popular subject for the cards. The size and prosperity of the locality were attested to by the success of its trolley operation, and often the trolley company would pull out as many cars as possible while photographs were being made of Main Street. Some postcard manufacturers were not above superimposing trolleys on Main Streets that never had them, drawing in tracks and overhead wires where none ever existed, just to make the town appear to be a little bigger and more important.

This collection of trolley postcards is limited to the United States (including Hawaii) and the Commonwealth of Puerto Rico. There were trolleys in every state but Alaska. The captions give the name of the trolley company in existence at the time the postcard was made. This has often been difficult to ascertain because many of the lines changed names and owners so frequently. In some cases the name is on the trolley in the picture, but sometimes the designation appears to be fictitious.

At the present time, collecting old postcards has become a big business with enormous profits for the dealers and middlemen. Prices are frequently prohibitive. Most collectors store their cards where they remain unseen by the public. All too often, even when a collection is left to a museum, it is stored away, or disappears by degrees, or else is sold off again for lack of interest. In book form, there is a better chance of preserving these cards for posterity so that future generations may enjoy a little of the flavor of the postcard and trolley era.

CHRONOLOGY OF THE POSTCARD

1869 Austria issued the first postcards.

1893 U.S. government (penny) postcards were put through the presses a second time, showing views of the Columbian Exposition in Chicago.

1898 By an act of Congress on May 19, private manufacturers were permitted to make postcards, with the back restricted to the address and stamp only. These were called "private mailing cards."

1901/2 The private mailing cards stopped, and regular 3½" x 5½" postcards started. The cards of this period are generally referred to as undivided backs, since the entire back was still reserved for address and stamp. It was about this time that the postcard craze began.

1907 On March 1, the Postmaster General permitted a line to be drawn on the back of postcards and a message to be written on the left side. At first this vertical line was somewhat to the left of center, allowing less room for the message, but a later rule permitted the line to be placed in the center. These cards became known as divided backs.

1914/17 After the outbreak of the First World War, the technically finest American-view postcards—those printed in Germany—were no longer available. Most postcards issued after this were American-made, and of poorer quality. They generally had a white border, and became known as white-border cards. After the United States entered the war, the postcard craze ended.

1930 A new type of card, the linen, was introduced, probably the ugliest and most grotesque ever made. The linen effect of the surface made all clarity of detail impossible. The colors were artificial and never attractive.

1940 The chrome card was introduced. It had a smooth, glossy finish, and was much clearer than the linens or the white-border cards, but the printed description was put on the back, making it much less attractive to the collector (this had been done sporadically earlier).

1970   A king-size chrome was introduced in Europe. It is now being
        used in the United States. The caption has returned to the pic-
        ture side, the picture is much clearer, and the size is generally 4″
        x 5⅞″. Most of the first of these new king-size cards in use here
        seem to have emanated from Dublin, Ireland.

1978   The king-sized chrome is now in general use everywhere and is
        manufactured everywhere. The cost is 10 to 15 cents, and occa-
        sionally a quarter, per card.

NOTE: The cards are arranged alphabetically by state and, within each state,
alphabetically by the locality actually depicted on the card. The captions begin with
the locality and state, immediately followed by the name of the trolley company
represented. The color section of 16 cards has a separate alphabetization of its own,
based on the same principles.

   Much of the information on miles of track and number of cars is drawn from
various issues of the semiannual *McGraw Electric Railway List,* McGraw-Hill, N.Y.
Many of the dates of termination of lines were obtained from Atwood's *Catalogue of
U.S. and Canadian Transportation Tokens.*

   Given in parentheses at the end of each caption is all the information available on
place of printing and/or publication of card, and date; ''n.d.'' indicates that the card
in question was never mailed.

Dexter Avenue looking east, Capitol in distance, Montgomery, Ala.

MONTGOMERY, ALABAMA. Montgomery Street Railway. This city was unique in having an electric trolley (Vandepoele type) as early as 1886, but in a year or two it reverted to mule traction. The line shown here, with 38 miles of track and 56 motor cars in 1914, leased Pickett Springs Park and owned Washington Park. (Printed in Germany)

PHOENIX, ARIZONA. Phoenix Railway Co. All the cars at this meet (transfer point) in the center of town appear to be of the California type (partially closed, either in the center only, or for half the length of the car). Phoenix had electric trolleys from 1893 to 1948. (Printed in Germany for M. Rieder, Los Angeles; postmarked May 19, 1908)

West Markham St. from Main St., Little Rock, Ark. 3874

LITTLE ROCK, ARKANSAS. Little Rock Railway & Electric Co. This line, which stayed within town, going as far as (company controlled) Forest Park, was large for the size of the city, with 43 miles of track and 92 motorized passenger cars in 1922. (Printed in Germany for I. Goodman, Little Rock; before 1907)

Double Deck Car at Coronado Tent City, Cal.

CORONADO, CALIFORNIA. Coronado Railroad. This line was later purchased by the San Diego Electric Railway Co. The car shown was probably the most beautiful double-decker ever to run in America. The lower section is a typical California-type trolley with open seats at either end; the upper deck is open with back-to-back lengthwise seats. (Printed in Germany for the Newman Post Card Co., Los Angeles; postmarked Dec. 5, 1908)

Pleasure Seekers arriving at Long Beach, Cal.

LONG BEACH, CALIFORNIA. Pacific Electric Railway Co. This mightiest of interurban fleets (some 720 passenger cars) connected Los Angeles with principal suburbs for 75 miles around, and owned the resort and funicular railway at Mount Lowe. (Printed in the U.S. for the Carlin Post Card Co., Los Angeles; n.d.)

LOS ANGELES, CALIFORNIA. Pacific Electric Railway Co.. The first trolley bus ever to operate commercially was in Laurel Canyon and was built to service a real-estate development called Bungalowland in the San Fernando Valley. One of the two trolley poles was a positive, the other a negative (on regular trolleys the track served as a negative). (Published by Jack Parsons, Los Angeles; n.d.)

6112. CIRCULAR BRIDGE. MT. LOWE RAILWAY. CAL.   ELEVATION 6000 FEET

MOUNT LOWE, CALIFORNIA. Mount Lowe Railway Co. People took this hair-raising ride long before the Pacific Electric Railway existed, as this early view shows. The motorman, his coat thrown over the front of the car, is working the hand brake. (Published by the Detroit Photographic Co. with an 1899 copyright)

Key Route, Ferry Pier, Oakland, Cal.

Photo only Copyrighted by M.Rieder, 1907

OAKLAND, CALIFORNIA. San Francisco-Oakland Terminal Railways. This line, equipped with pantographs instead of poles on most of its 380 motor cars, was known as the "Key System" and ran from Oakland to Alameda, Berkeley, Richmond, Albany, San Leandro, Hayward and Piedmont. It also owned five ferryboats making the run to San Francisco, and the pier on the card was the trolley terminus. (Printed in Germany for M. Rieder, Los Angeles, with a 1907 copyright)

Orange and Santa Ana Motor, Cal.

ORANGE, CALIFORNIA. Orange & Santa Ana Motor Co. In this steam trolley, the fireman sat in the central enclosure and the motorman could do little other than stop the car. The card dates from about 1908, but the very detailed photo may be earlier. (Printed in Germany for M. Rieder, Los Angeles; n.d.)

1803 – ON THE WAY TO PASADENA, CALIFORNIA, ON PACIFIC ELECTRIC RAILWAY.

PASADENA, CALIFORNIA. Pacific Electric Railway Co. Even this great trolley line had to bow to the whims of the railroads and use this two-track wooden bridge over the railroad track. The manufacturer of this card, who was possibly America's best, never published subjects east of the Rockies. (Printed in the U.S. for Edward H. Mitchell, San Francisco; n.d.)

5

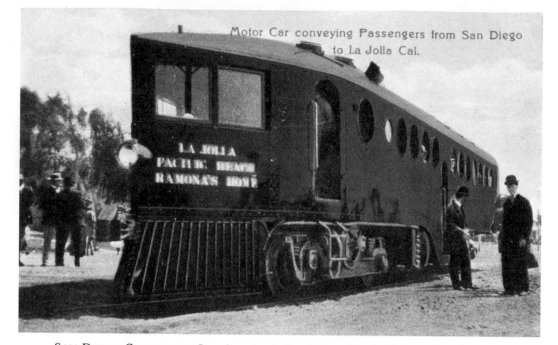

SAN DIEGO, CALIFORNIA. Los Angeles & San Diego Beach Railway Co. Called a McKeen car, this cross between a trolley and a train operated on gasoline power on tracks. It was used in many parts of the country. Despite its name, the line ran from San Diego to La Jolla only. (Printed in Germany for the Newman Post Card Co., Los Angeles; n.d.)

SAN FRANCISCO, CALIFORNIA. Market Street Railway Co. This line, a successor to United Railroads of San Francisco, had 295 miles and 847 trolleys. It was purchased by the city in 1922. (Printed in Germany for the Pacific Novelty Co., San Francisco; n.d.)

UPLAND, CALIFORNIA. Ontario & San Antonio Heights Rail Road Co., Los Angeles. This line was a predecessor of the Pacific Electric Railway Co. After the horse or mule pulled the car uphill it had a free ride down on a trailer in the back. (''Photochrom'' card of the C.T. Co., Chicago; photo dated 1895)

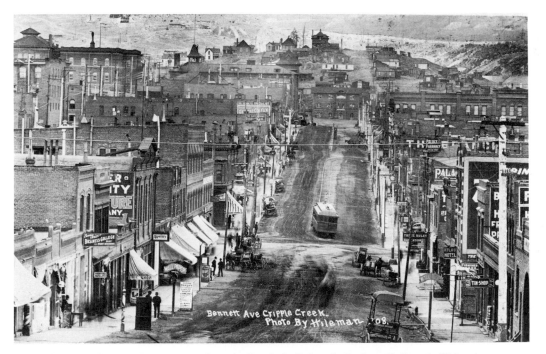

CRIPPLE CREEK, COLORADO. Cripple Creek & Colorado Springs Railroad. This company, begun in 1897, had two lines to the goldfields, the Low Line and the High Line, the latter going by way of mountains up to more than 10,000 feet above sea level. The total trackage was only 18½ miles and there were only 11 cars in all. After the gold rush ended, this line folded up in 1922. (Original-photograph card; photo by Hileman dated 1908)

DERBY, CONNECTICUT. The Connecticut Co. (Bridgeport Division). The car is bound for Bridgeport. (Printed in Germany for the Howard & Barber Co., Derby; n.d.)

NEW HAVEN, CONNECTICUT. The Connecticut Co. (New Haven Division). This early cross-bench open car with single truck and Bombay (or ''turtleback'') roof is bound for Horton St. The New Haven was the last Connecticut Co. division to run trolleys—until September 25, 1948. (Printed in Great Britain for Valentine, published by the Globe Art Co., Stamford, Conn.; n.d.)

Franklin Square looking E., Norwich, Conn.

NORWICH, CONNECTICUT. Norwich & Westerly Traction Co. The car at the lower left is bound for Westerly, the middle one is a local Connecticut Co. trolley bound for Taftville and the third is an oversize Connecticut Co. car going to Putnam and Grosvenor Dale. All of these lines were absorbed into the Shore Line Electric Railway Co. for some years. (Printed in England for E. A. Bardol & Co., Norwich; n.d.)

TROLLEY TERMINAL, PLAINVILLE, CONN.

PLAINVILLE, CONNECTICUT. Connecticut Railway & Lighting Co. Note the gates for the railroad tracks and the horse-drawn delivery wagon with the umbrella to protect the driver. (Original-photograph card published by the J. C. Dexter Photo Co., Hartford, Conn. before 1907)

THOMPSONVILLE, CONNECTICUT. Hartford & Springfield Street Railway Co. This is undoubtedly a special car for some outing. The line, with 48 miles of track, also ran to Rockville, Ellington and Somers, across to the west side of the Connecticut River and up north to Suffield. All of this was abandoned in 1926. (Postmarked Apr. 9, 1912)

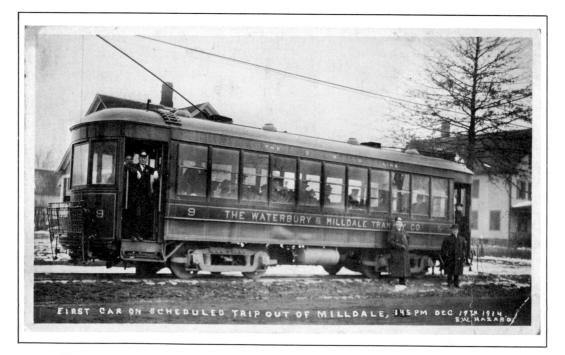

WATERBURY, CONNECTICUT. Waterbury & Milldale Tramway Co. This was an independent line, and the card commemorates the first nine-mile trip from Milldale to Waterbury. (Original-photograph card; photo by E. W. Hazard dated 1914)

WINSTED, CONNECTICUT. Consolidated Railway Co. This is a view on the way to Highland Lake Park. This line, which ran about 13 miles and had 26 cars in 1918, may even have become the Torrington Division of the Connecticut Co. before this card was printed. (Postmarked Aug. 27, 1907)

WILMINGTON, DEL.   8th and Market Sts.

WILMINGTON, DELAWARE. Wilmington & Philadelphia Traction Co. This interurban line connected not only the name cities, but also Media and Chester in Pennsylvania, and New Castle and Delaware City in Delaware. (''Peacock'' card printed in the U.S.; before 1907)

WASHINGTON, DISTRICT OF COLUMBIA. Capital Traction Co. Pennsylvania Avenue is being paved in this view. The slot between the running rails was the power pickup, or underground third rail, required by law in the District of Columbia (as also in Manhattan and Paris). When this line crossed into Maryland, a man in a pit under the trolley made the switchover from the third rail to overhead wiring. (Original-photograph card; photo dated 1912)

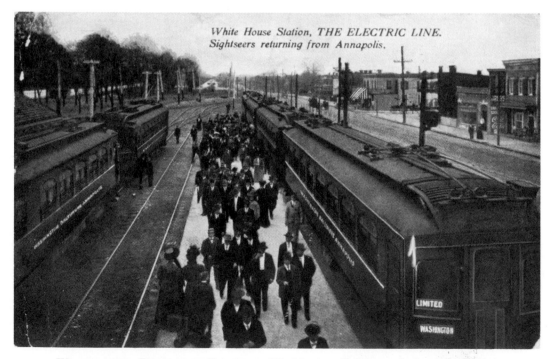

WASHINGTON, DISTRICT OF COLUMBIA. Washington, Baltimore & Annnapolis Electric Railway Co., Baltimore. The trains on this interurban were up to six cars long. In 1914 there were 111 miles of track and 28 motorized passenger cars. The round trip for the tour to Annapolis was $1.50. (Printed locally as an ad for the line; postmarked May 12, 1909)

Copyright 1905 by the Rotograph Co.

10362 Main Entrance.

The Florida Ostrich Farm, Jacksonville

JACKSONVILLE, FLORIDA. Jacksonville Electric Co. (or San Jose Traction Co.). Both of the lines named were out of business by 1919. This was a five-foot (wide-gauge) line 60 miles long. (Printed in Germany for the Rotograph Co., N.Y.; photo dated 1905)

12TH STREET FROM AVENUE D., LOOKING EAST, MIAMI, FLA.

MIAMI, FLORIDA. Miami Traction Co. The battery-powered car is operating on what later became Flagler St. Miami's first streetcar line had run about three miles in 1905/6. The Miami Traction Co., 1914–1921, was the second, running five miles to Tatum Park, which it owned. In 1922 it was bought by the city and leased to the Miami Beach Electric Co. (Printed in the U.S. for the H. & W. B. Drew Co., Jacksonville; n.d.)

PALM BEACH, FLORIDA. Florida East Coast Co. (?). These mule cars would go from one plush hotel to another on the island of Palm Beach, such as The Breakers, shown here. (Printed in Frankfurt, Germany for the Hugh C. Leighton Co., Portland, Me.; n.d.)

ST. AUGUSTINE, FLORIDA. St. Augustine & South Beach Railway. This unusual open-bench car evidently had an aisle down the middle so that one could enter from the side as well as from the front platform. It ran to Anastasia and to the company's two parks, South Beach and Chautauqua Beach. (Printed in Germany for Allen, St. Augustine; postmarked Mar. 31, 1909)

SANFORD, FLORIDA. Sanford Traction Co. Chiefly a freight line (dubbed the ''Celery Belt Line'')—in 1908 only, it carried schoolchildren—its two cars were gasoline-powered and gave constant mechanical trouble. (Printed in the U.S. for Cochrane's Book Store, Palatka, Fla.; n.d.)

ATLANTA, GEORGIA. Georgia Railway & Power Co. This company controlled most of the electric car lines in the area. In 1918 it had about 300 miles of track and a total of 412 cars of various kinds. (''Litho-Chrome'' card printed in Germany for the Georgia News Co., Atlanta; postmark illegible)

GAINESVILLE, GEORGIA. Gainesville Railway & Power Co. This line ran from Gainesville through New Holland to Chattahoochee Park. ("Peacock" card printed in Germany for Robertson & Law, Gainesville; n.d.)

SAVANNAH, GEORGIA. Savannah Electric Co. This system, with 59 miles of wide-gauge track and 75 motor cars in 1918, ran to Thunderbolt and Isle of Hope. The company did most of the electric light and power business in the area. (Printed in Great Britain for the Valentine & Sons' Publishing Co., N.Y.; n.d.)

HONOLULU, HAWAII. Honolulu Rapid Transit Co. In 1918, this line already had a bus in addition to its 54 trolleys with 30 miles of narrow-gauge (four-foot) track. (Original-photograph card; ca. 1915)

SHOSHONE FALLS, IDAHO. Twin Falls Railroad Co. This was one of the two Beach-Edison battery cars that did the 12 miles between Twin Falls and Shoshone Falls. They were discontinued about 1920. (Original-photograph card published by the Pacific Photo Co., Salem, Ore.; n.d.)

Illinois Central Electric Railway, Canton, Ill.

CANTON, ILLINOIS. Illinois Central Electric Railway Co. This line, centered in Canton, connected Farmington and Lewistown. With 83 miles of track, it had only six trolleys; perhaps the trailers were borrowed for an excursion. (Postmarked Oct. 14, 1908)

Trolley Bridge to Campbell's Island, near Moline, Ill.

MOLINE, ILLINOIS. Tri-City Railway Co. of Illinois, Rock Island. This 42-mile line, which connected Rock Island, Moline, Sears and Milan, owned Watch Tower Park in Rock Island and the 275-acre Campbell's Island on the Illinois side of the Mississippi. (Probably printed in the U.S.; n.d.)

TERMINAL TRAIN SHED, INDIANAPOLIS, IND.   10073

INDIANAPOLIS, INDIANA. Indianapolis & Cincinnati Traction Co. This was probably the country's greatest interurban terminal. Opened in 1904, it handled as many as 500 big interurban cars a day, with freight handled elsewhere. The last interurban reached the terminal on January 18, 1941. (Printed in Germany for A. C. Bosselman & Co., N.Y.; postmarked Sept. 14, 1908)

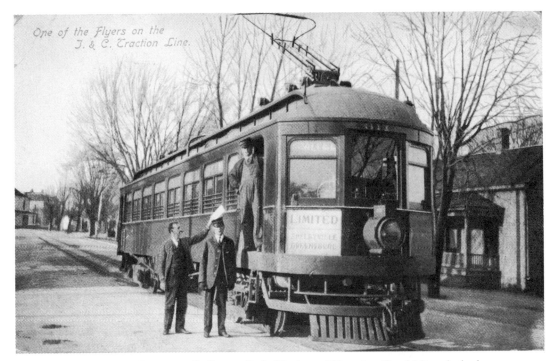

One of the Flyers on the
J. & C. Traction Line.

INDIANAPOLIS, INDIANA. Indianapolis & Cincinnati Traction Co. Although the bow, with which this interurban is picking up power from the overhead wire, was and is in common use in Europe, it was a rarity in the United States. (Printed in Germany for the Indiana News Co., Indianapolis; n.d.)

B. & O. and Interurban Crossing, Milford Jct., Ind.

MILFORD JUNCTION, INDIANA. Winona Interurban Railway Co., Warsaw, Ind. The railroad tracks are those of the Baltimore & Ohio. Grade crossings between railroads and trolley lines, especially the fast interurbans, were very rare. (No place, no date)

The Bearss Hotel, Peru, Ind.

PERU, INDIANA. Indiana Union Traction Co. There is no record of this line, although the car—grotesquely large for a city street—is thus labeled. (Printed in the U.S.; ca. 1910)

South Shore Interurban Cars.

SOUTH BEND, INDIANA. Chicago, Lake Shore & South Bend Railway Co., Michigan City, Ind. The line is still in operation. Note the pantographs and trolley poles. The two-car train is probably waiting at a turnout for another interurban to come through from the opposite direction. (Printed in the U.S. for H. W. Lewis, South Bend; postmarked South Bend, Apr. 19, 1910)

Union Park
Waiting Station, Dubuque.

DUBUQUE, IOWA. Dubuque Electric Co. Owned by the company (as was Nutwood Park), 83-acre Union Park offered a variety of amusements. (Printed in the U.S. for the B. B. Co.; n.d.)

OSKALOOSA, IOWA. Oskaloosa Traction & Light Co. With nine miles of track and 14 cars, this company also supplied electric light and owned a subsidiary trolley line. (Printed in Germany for John T. Faber, Milwaukee; postmarked Apr. 11, 1908)

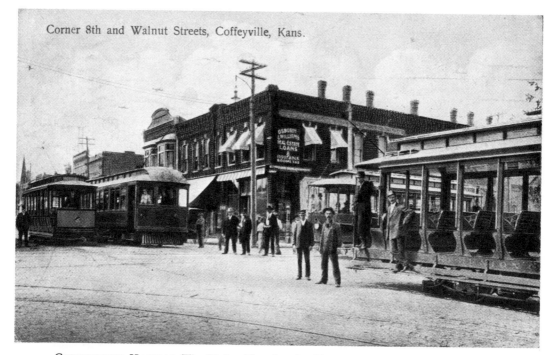

COFFEYVILLE, KANSAS. The Union Traction Co. The little city of Coffeyville was the center of a large interurban line that included 23 miles of track in Oklahoma. At least three different types of cars are shown at this meet. (Printed in Germany for the International Post Card Co., N.Y.; postmarked May 21, 1909)

HUTCHINSON, KANSAS. Hutchinson Inter-Urban Railway Co. The card commemorates the opening of the line on September 1, 1906. The town politicians in
the main car are followed by a brass band in the trailer. The line never ran more than
the 13 miles to the State Fair grounds and Stevens Park. (Original-photograph card;
photo by Samuel Hirst dated 1906; postmarked Oct. 5, 1906)

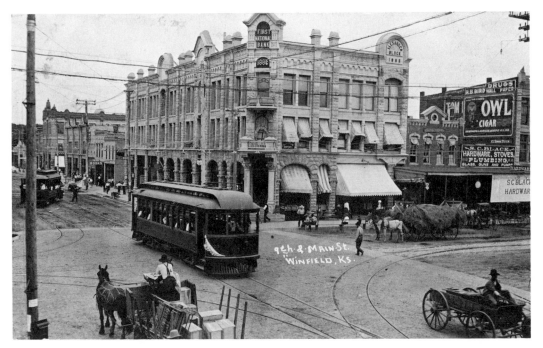

WINFIELD, KANSAS. Southwestern Interurban Railway Co. The line, which ran some
25 miles to Hackney and Arkansas City, had only five trolleys by 1922. (Original-
photograph card; postmarked July 19, 1910)

BARBOURVILLE TRACTION SYSTEM, BARBOURVILLE, KY.

BARBOURVILLE, KENTUCKY. Barbourville Traction System. The driver of the mule in this picture is a woman. Most horsecars had been converted to electricity long before this card was mailed. ("Doubletone" card of the C. T. Co., Chicago; postmarked Feb. 6, 1917)

MAIN STREET, LOOKING WEST FROM ANN STREET, FRANKFORT, KY.

FRANKFORT, KENTUCKY. Kentucky Traction & Terminal Co., Lexington. This company also operated city lines in Paris, Winchester and Georgetown. (White-border "American Art" card of the C. T. Co., Chicago; postmarked July 13, 1920)

COEUR D'ALENE, IDAHO. Spokane & Inland Empire Rail Road Co. This was the Idaho terminal of one of the most picturesque interurbans in the West. The cars always ran as trains, three or four together. This division of the line (steam and electric) ran 58 miles from Spokane, and carried the mail; the other went from Spokane to Colfax, Washington. (Spokane Post Card Co.; n.d.)

CHICAGO, ILLINOIS. Chicago Surface Lines. About 50 trolleys are backed up on Dearborn St. in this automobile-less traffic jam. The last trolley in Chicago ran on the Clark-Wentworth line on June 22, 1958. (V. O. Hammon Publishing Co., Chicago; n.d.)

INDIANAPOLIS, INDIANA. Indianapolis Traction & Terminal Co. In 1902 this company leased the Indianapolis Street Railway Co. for 31 years, but the lease ended in 1922, probably because of bankruptcy. In 1918 there were 141 miles of track, 564 motor cars and 84 other cars. (Printed in Leipzig for W. G. MacFarlane, Toronto; n.d.)

BOSTON, MASSACHUSETTS. Boston Elevated Railway Co. This subway entrance was used from 1897 to 1914 for points west of the Public Garden. The tunnel was extended several times until it reached Kenmore by 1922, but by that time the open cars were gone. (''Phostint'' card printed and published by the Detroit Publishing Co.; postmarked Apr. 29, 1913)

12964   LEAVING LOWER STATION FOR SUMMIT, MT. TOM RAILWAY, HOLYOKE, MASS.   DETROIT PUBLISHING CO.

HOLYOKE, MASSACHUSETTS. Mount Tom Rail Road Co. This was one of the two cars, balanced by a cable, on the electric incline railway from Mountain Park (owned by the Holyoke Street Railway Co.) to the top of Mount Tom. The two cars passed in opposite directions at a turnout halfway up. (''Phostint'' card printed and published by the Detroit Publishing Co.; postmarked Aug. 28, 1909)

Walnut Street Looking North from Tenth, Kansas City, Mo.

KANSAS CITY, MISSOURI. Kansas City Railways Co. (Fall Bros., Kansas City, probably printed in the U.S.; postmarked Apr. 6, 1921)

OMAHA, NEBRASKA. Omaha & Council Bluffs Street Railway Co. Only two automobiles are visible in this crowded scene with three policemen directing traffic (ca. 1910).

NEW YORK, NEW YORK. New York Railways Co. This company introduced the type of surface car seen here, the "hobble-skirt" car, in 1914. The doors were at the center, with steps only six inches from the ground to accommodate the long, tight skirts of the period. After entering there was another step up to get into either end of the car. (Printed and published by the American Art Publishing Co., N.Y.; n.d., but the plays advertised were running in the late winter and spring of 1914)

TROY, NEW YORK. Cohoes Railroad Co. (or United Traction Co.). Troy was served by many lines (from 1892 to 1934) and had more beautiful trolley postcards than any other city of its size in America. (Printed in Great Britain for Valentine & Sons' Publishing Co., N.Y.; n.d.)

ASHEVILLE, NORTH CAROLINA. Asheville Power & Light Co. The four-wheel cars in this view of about 1910 were part of the local line serving Asheville and its suburbs. (Printed in thē U.S. for Brown Book Co., Asheville; n.d.)

EAST LIVERPOOL, OHIO. East Liverpool Traction & Light Co. This is a typical example of a daylight scene artificially darkened to represent night—although the shadows and the mid-afternoon hour on the clock remain! ("Newvochrome" card printed in Germany; postmarked Nov. 13, 1912)

Broadway, Providence, R. I.

PROVIDENCE, RHODE ISLAND. Rhode Island Co. The motorman has no protection from the elements in this pre-labor union period (this card was made between 1908 and 1911). (Printed in Germany for the Rhode Island News Co., Providence; n.d.)

P. AND N. TRAIN AT CHICK SPRINGS, NEAR GREENVILLE. S. C.

GREENVILLE, SOUTH CAROLINA. Piedmont & Northern Railways Co., Charlotte, N.C. This line was a merger of two separate divisions never physically joined: the Greenville, Spartanburg & Anderson Railway Co., and the Piedmont Traction Co. More an electric railroad than a trolley line, this interurban had dining, observation and even sleeping cars. (White-border card printed in the U.S. after 1914 for the Southern Post Card Co., Asheville, N.C.; n.d.)

OLD TREE, RIVER AVENUE, SAN ANTONIO, TEXAS

SAN ANTONIO, TEXAS. San Antonio Traction Co. The gaint oak featured on the card, then already 150 to 200 years old, was close to Breckenridge Park. The trolley line, which ran from West End Lake to Alamo Heights, was taken over in 1917 by the San Antonio Public Service Co. (Printed in Germany for Geo. M. Bearce, San Antonio; n.d.)

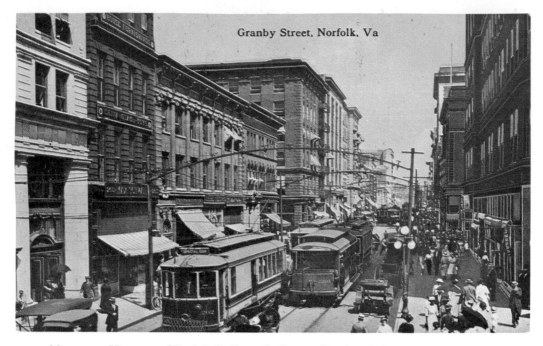

Granby Street, Norfolk, Va

NORFOLK, VIRGINIA. Virginia Railway & Power Co. (Norfolk Division). This line connected Norfolk with Newport News, Portsmouth and other localities. (Printed in the U.S. for Louis Kaufmann & Sons, Baltimore; n.d.)

YAKIMA, WASHINGTON. Yakima Interurban Trolley Lines (restored). This is *1776,* one of the two 1906 trolleys purchased from Oporto, Portugal (the other is *1976*) to celebrate the Bicentennial. Yakima, the first town to restore old trolleys, fortunately had never removed the 21 miles of overhead wire. (Modern ''chrome'' postcard printed by Dexter Press, West Nyack, N.Y., published by Ken Whitmire Associates, Yakima; n.d.)

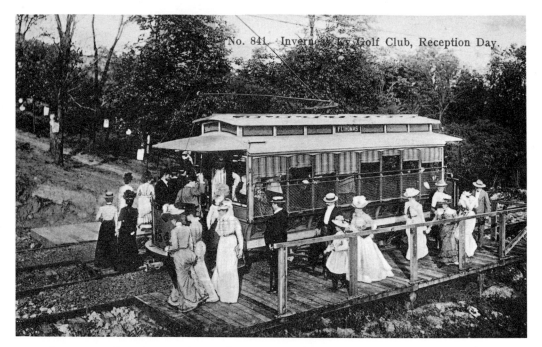

INVERNESS, KENTUCKY. South Covington & Cincinnati Street Railway Co., Covington. The apparently open car is really a convertible with a center aisle. This was the only trolley line operating in two states that had different requirements about overhead wiring, Cincinnati being the only American city in which both positive and negative contacts had to be overhead (as also in Havana and Tokyo). (Printed in Germany for the Kraemer Art Co., Cincinnati; n.d.)

NEW ORLEANS, LOUISIANA. New Orleans Railway & Light Co. Canal St., the widest street in America, had four and sometimes five parallel trolley tracks. The line had 218 miles of track, 584 motor cars and 108 other cars in 1918. Trolleys are still being operated as a museum attraction on St. Charles Ave. (Printed in Frankfurt, Germany for the H. C. Leighton Co., Portland, Me.; n.d.)

Noon Hour,
Pepperel Mfg, Co.,
Biddeford, Me.

BIDDEFORD, MAINE. Biddeford & Saco Rail Road Co. The open car was used in the summer to take the factory hands to and from work. There were 22 trolleys on eight miles of track. When the line closed in 1939, the Seashore Trolley Museum, five miles away, was established and its first acquisition was a car like the one in the picture. (No place, no date)

BRUNSWICK, MAINE. Lewiston, Augusta & Waterville Street Railway Co. The company, a consolidation of many smaller lines, was itself reorganized into the Androscoggin & Kennebec Street Railway Co. in 1919. The most beautiful parlor car ever used in Maine, the *Merrymeeting* took special parties on excursions. (''Photochrom'' card of the C. T. Co., Chicago, published by James F. Snow, Brunswick; n.d.)

"The Oxford" where the Fryeburg fire of Aug. 31st started.

FRYEBURG, MAINE. Fryeburg Horse Rail Road Co. This three-mile, six-car line, never electrified, was suspended in 1917. The hotel fire in the picture took place in 1907. (Postmarked Sept. 13, 1907)

Depot Square, Gardiner, Me.

GARDINER, MAINE. Augusta, Winthrop & Gardiner Railroad Co. The trolley is of the single-truck open-bench variety, and the covered bridge crosses the Kennebec River. The line was later absorbed into the Lewiston, Augusta & Waterville Street Railway Co. (Printed in Germany for Robbins Bros., Boston; ca. 1907)

LEWISTON, MAINE. Lewiston, Augusta & Waterville Street Railway Co. The car in the foreground with the large observation rear platform is bound for Waterville, some 40 miles away. The little open car was called the ''Figure Eight'' because it made two loops through Lewiston and Auburn. The third car is headed in a different direction, for Bath, 25 miles away on the coast. (Printed in the U.S.; postmark year unclear)

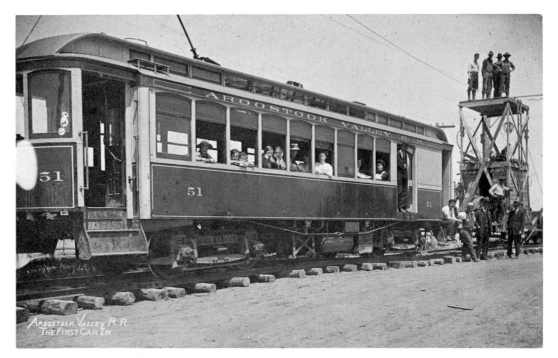

NEW SWEDEN, MAINE. Aroostook Valley Rail Road Co., Presque Isle. Despite the ''51'' on the car, it was one of just four on this 38-mile line in northern Maine. The picture was taken right after the trolley line had beaten the railroad to New Sweden in a tracklaying race for the franchise. (Original-photograph card; postmarked Sept. 26, 1911)

PORTLAND, MAINE. Portland Railroad Co. The trolley company owned Riverton Park, where this crowd is gathered, and Cape Cottage Park. (Printed in Frankfurt, Germany for the Hugh C. Leighton Co., Portland; postmarked Sept. 5, 1909)

ROCKLAND, MAINE. Rockland, Thomaston & Camden Street Railway Co. The conductor is standing at the controls (at the rear of the car in this instance) and the man on the ground is the motorman, waiting for the car from the opposite direction. (Original-photograph card; postmarked Oct. 9, 1909)

YORK, MAINE. Atlantic Shore Line Railway. This large open car of the double-truck type is crossing Sewall's Bridge, called on the card the "first pile bridge built in America" and dated 1761. ("Phostint" card of the Detroit Publishing Co.; dated 1908)

YORK BEACH, MAINE. Atlantic Shore Line Railway. At Kittery, the vacationers in this open car will transfer to the company-owned ferry (one of the few in America owned by a trolley line) to go to Portsmouth, N.H. (Printed in Frankfurt, Germany for the Hugh C. Leighton Co., Portland, Me.; postmarked Aug. 21, 1909)

"TOONERVILLE TROLLEY." NORTH BEACH, MD.

NORTH BEACH, MARYLAND. "Toonerville Trolley." North Beach is on the west side of Chesapeake Bay, about 30 miles southeast of Washington. It apparently never had a trolley line, yet the card shows a single-truck open-bench horsecar seemingly pushed by a gasoline tractor on rails. (Postmarked Oct. 18, 1922)

The Shopping Hour, Washington Street, Boston, Mass.

211,799 (JV)

BOSTON, MASSACHUSETTS. Boston Elevated Railway Co. The card shows the busy shopping street in front of the famous Jordan Marsh department store. (Printed in the U.S. for the Leighton & Valentine Co., N.Y.; postmarked Dec. 14, 1911)

BOSTON, MASSACHUSETTS. Boston Elevated Railway Co. No autos are in sight in this 1907 view. The structure in the middle of the square is a subway entrance. (Printed in the U.S. for the Souvenir Post Card Co.; n.d.)

BOSTON, MASSACHUSETTS. Boston Elevated Railway Co. Boston had trolleys on the ground, in subway tunnels and on elevated tracks. Dudley St. Station, where there was a transfer between trolleys and el trains, was also the starting point for many trolleys going to the south of Boston. (Detroit Publishing Co.; dated 1904)

BUCKLAND, MASSACHUSETTS. Shelburne Falls & Colerain Street Railway Co. Built in 1908, the cement bridge from Shelburne Falls to Buckland over which this combination passenger and freight car is seen passing, still exists today, as the water mains to Buckland are embedded in it. It is now called ''The Bridge of Flowers.'' (Original-photograph card; n.d.)

HOLBROOK, MASSACHUSETTS. Brockton Street Railway Co. This line later went through several name changes. The car shown is said to be the first operated in Holbrook in 1892. (Printed in Brooklyn, N.Y. for Charles W. Lincoln; postmarked Mar. 18, 1908)

Post Office and Red Men's Hall, Lyonsville, Mass.

LYONSVILLE, MASSACHUSETTS. Shelburne Falls & Colerain Street Railway Co. This beautiful little four-wheel open car connected the two towns in the company's title. (Printed in Germany for W. B. Hale, Williamsville, Mass.; n.d.)

Newton Square facing Galon Street, Newton, Mass.

60016

NEWTON, MASSACHUSETTS. Middlesex & Boston Street Railway Co., Newtonville. This is the line of the single-truck trolley at the left, with its sign ''Moody, High and Crafts Sts.'' The other two cars may belong to the Boston & Worcester Street Railway Co. of Boston. (''Souvochrome'' card printed in N.Y. for the Souvenir Post Card Co.; postmarked Mar. 6, 1916)

34

Entrance to Orient Springs, Pelham, Mass.

PELHAM, MASSACHUSETTS. Holyoke Street Railway Co. Orient Springs, four miles east of Amherst, was a picnic site. The 14-mile ride from Holyoke took an hour and five minutes and cost 16 cents. The line was electrified in 1895 and ran until 1937. ("Litho-Chrome" card printed in Germany for C. E. Ewell, Amherst; postmark unclear)

PARLOR CAR "BERKSHIRE HILLS"—(EXTERIOR VIEW)

SCHEDULE DAILY, INCLUDING SUNDAY

Northbound—Read Down		Southbound—Read Up
A.M.		P.M.
*7.39	Lv. Great Barrington	Ar. 6.51
8.23	Stockbridge	Lv. 6.07
8.45	Lee Center	5.45
9.00	Lenox Station	5.30
9.25	Ar. Pittsfield	5.05
9.53	Lv. Pittsfield	Ar. 4.38
11.15	North Adams	3.15
11.37	Williamstown Sta.	2.52
12.12 P.M.	Ar. Bennington	Lv.*2.18

TICKETS ON SALE—Berkshire Inn, Gt. Barrington; Wendell Hotel, Pittsfield; Red Lion Inn, Stockbridge; Richmond Hotel, No. Adams; Greenock Inn, Lee Ctr.; Putnam Hotel, Ben'gton, Vt.

PITTSFIELD, MASSACHUSETTS. Berkshire Street Railway Co. Probably the finest parlor car ever, built at a cost of some $20,000, the excursion trolley *Berkshire Hills* is here shown still at the factory. Sold as a diner for $400, the car is now embedded in the framework of a fancy restaurant west of Pittsfield. (No place, no date)

South River Station

SOUTH RIVER, MASSACHUSETTS. Conway Electric Street Railway Co. This little isolated line (6.6 miles, five trolleys) connected the New York, New Haven & Hartford station with the Boston & Maine station at South River. Its freight operation was apparently most important, but it also had an electric park called Wildwood Park. (Printed in Germany for W. W. Darby; postmarked Aug. 24, 1916)

11789 MASSASOIT HOUSE AND R. R. ARCH, SPRINGFIELD, MASS.

SPRINGFIELD, MASSACHUSETTS. Springfield Street Railway Co. The arch in the picture carried the main line of the Boston & Albany Railroad. The trolley line operated 191 miles of track and had 474 cars of all kinds in 1918. (''Phostint'' card of the Detroit Publishing Co.; n.d.)

36

CARLOW'S CORNER, TAUNTON, MASS.

TAUNTON, MASSACHUSETTS. East Taunton Street Railway Co. and Bay State Street Railway Co. The car on the left is a local trolley; the one on the right is a Bay State car (main office, Boston) bound for Brockton. Trolleys ran in Taunton from 1893 to 1932. (Printed in Germany for Henry A. Dickerman & Son, Taunton; postmarked Sept. 29, 1910)

Tech. Special Car, Worcester, Mass.

WORCESTER, MASSACHUSETTS. Worcester Polytechnic Institute. This car, used by the engineering school for education and experimental work, was not owned by any trolley line but moved freely throughout the trolley world. (Souvenir Post Card Co. card; postmarked June 25, 1914)

BERRIEN SPRINGS, MICHIGAN. Southern Michigan Railway Co., South Bend, Ind. This line connected South Bend with several cities in Michigan. The bridge in the picture, over the St. Joseph River, was the longest interurban trolley bridge in the world, 1600 feet, with eight spans. (Original-photograph card; no place or date)

DETROIT, MICHIGAN. Detroit United Railway. A typical big-city sightseeing car (these usually had ''barkers'' calling out the sights), the *Yolande* seems to have had a lavatory (shaded window). (Printed in Germany for the Rotograph Co., N.Y.; postmark illegible)

GRAND HAVEN, MICHIGAN. Grand Rapids, Grand Haven & Muskegon Railway Co. This line served the communities in its name and owned the great Pomona Pleasure Park in Fruitport. The Gildner Hotel stage is seen leaving for the depot. (Printed in Milwaukee for the E. C. Kropf Co.; n.d.)

MENOMINEE, MICHIGAN. Menominee & Marinette Light & Traction Co. This little interstate line ran between the two cities in Michigan and Wisconsin. It also owned the local electric light and gas companies and Lakeside Park in Marinette. (Printed in Germany for the Kirkham Photograph Studio, Menominee; postmarked Oct. 4, 1907)

MONROE, MICHIGAN. Detroit, Monroe & Toledo Short Line Railroad Co. The car on the left is a convertible with 16 windows and a deck roof. The other is a normal-sized closed car with a railroad roof. (''Peacock'' card printed in Germany for F. I. A. Mitchell, Monroe; postmarked Sept. 15, 1908)

MINNEAPOLIS, MINNESOTA. Twin City Rapid Transit Co. This large city line manufactured all its own streetcars, a rather unusual procedure. The cars, distinguished by their right rear-corner doors, were not reversible and each terminus required a loop to turn them around. (''Phostint'' card of the Detroit Publishing Co., dated 1908; postmarked Aug. 10, 1908)

Intersection of 14th and 25th Avenue,
Gulfport, Miss.

GULFPORT, MISSISSIPPI. Gulfport & Mississippi Coast Traction Co. The line ran along the shore road on the Gulf of Mexico, and went through Biloxi as far west as Pass Christian. (''Photochrom'' card of the C. T. Co., Chicago; n.d.)

"Where Gulf Breezes Frolic."

This Car Traverses Twenty-eight Miles of Scenic Beauty along the Gulf Beach with The Great Southern Hotel in the Center, Gulfport, Miss.

GULFPORT, MISSISSIPPI. Gulfport & Mississippi Coast Traction Co. The 30-mile line owned 20 motor and two trailer cars. (Probably printed in the U.S.; bears symbol of a Maltese cross with an eye in the center and a ''C'' on each spoke; postmarked Mar. 2, 1912)

Capital Street, looking East from Governor's Mansion, Jackson, Miss,

JACKSON, MISSISSIPPI. Jackson Light & Traction Co. This firm also supplied the city's electric light and gas. The state capitol can be seen at the end of the dirt road. (Printed in Germany for the Souvenir Post Card Co., N.Y.; n.d.)

Corner Oak & Magnolia Sts., Laurel, Miss.

LAUREL, MISSISSIPPI. Laurel Light & Railway Co. Three cars occupy a lot of space at this meet, but the 14-mile line had only eleven passenger cars in all in 1918. (No place, no date)

YAZOO CITY, MISSISSIPPI. Municipal Street Railway. Five cars ran on this four-mile line. (Printed in Germany for W. T. Hegman & Son, Yazoo City; n.d.)

Entrance, Lakeside Park, Carterville, Mo.

CARTERSVILLE, MISSOURI. Southwest Missouri Railway Co., Webb City. This line, which also serviced Joplin, Missouri and Galena, Kansas, owned the amusement park in the picture. ("Litho-Chrome" card printed in Germany for the P. O. Book Store, Cartersville; postmarked Dec. 5, 1907)

KANSAS CITY, MISSOURI. Kansas City Railways Co. This was a company formed by the merger of several others in 1916, actually later than the manufacture of this card. Many individual lines, and even an elevated railway, set out from Kansas City. (Postmarked Jan. 18, 1915)

KANSAS CITY, MISSOURI. Kansas City, Clay County & St. Joseph Railway Co. This trolley is an excellent example of the ''hobble-skirt'' type with low doors in the center. (Printed in the U.S. for Hall Bros., Kansas City; postmarked May 26, 1916)

28th Street, looking North,
Billings, Mont.

BILLINGS, MONTANA. Billings Traction Co. This storage-battery line, which had six cars and ran six miles, disappeared by 1920. (Bloom Bros., Minneapolis card, printed in the U.S., published for the Post Office News Stand, Billings; postmarked Nov. 20, 1912)

Sightseers at Columbia Gardens, Butte, Mont.

"SEEING BUTTE" Observation Car.

BUTTE, MONTANA. Butte Electric Railway Co. This was their sightseeing car. Columbia Gardens was an electric park owned by the trolley company. Butte had electric cars from 1890 to 1937. (Printed in Germany for the American Import Co., Minneapolis; n.d.)

Ore Conveying by Electricity, BUTTE, Mont.

BUTTE, MONTANA. Butte, Anaconda & Pacific Railway Co. Not a passenger operation, this freight line ran between Anaconda and Butte with 28 electric and 21 steam cars. In the background (far left) is a regular trolley of the Butte Electric Railway Co. (Printed in Germany for W. G. McFarlane, N.Y.; postmarked Feb. 12, 1914)

Montana's first Interurban at Salesville, Mont.

SALESVILLE, MONTANA. Gallatin Valley Railway, Bozeman. The car shown was the line's one combination car; there were also four passenger cars, one freight car and two steam locomotives. The 20-mile line was only partially electrified. (Published by the Wisey Mercantile Co., Salesville; postmarked Dec. 5, 1910)

O. Street, Looking East from 10th. Street, Lincoln, Neb.

Frank Du Teil,—Dist. Lincoln, Neb.

LINCOLN, NEBRASKA. Lincoln Traction Co. The early-model single-truck open car was built about 1908. The company connected Lincoln with several other towns. (''Elite'' card printed in Germany for the Suhling & Koehn Co., Chicago; n.d.)

New Court House and Riverside Hotel, Reno, Nev.

RENO, NEVADA. Reno Traction Co. The doors of these odd cars were about one-third way from either end. The line ran seven miles to Sparks between 1905 and 1927. (Printed in the U.S.; n.d.)

Tremont Square, Claremont, N. H.

CLAREMONT, NEW HAMPSHIRE. Claremont Railway & Lighting Co. The track of this little line is still intact through all the streets of Claremont, and is used for diesel-powered freight deliveries by the Claremont & Concord Railroad. (''Newvochrome'' card printed in Germany for the Springfield News Co., Springfield, Mass.; postmarked July 29, 1911)

HAMPTON BEACH, NEW HAMPSHIRE. Exeter, Hampton & Amesbury Street Railway Co. When this line folded it was taken over by the Exeter Railway & Light Co. and later by the town of Hampton. (Original-photograph card; photo by J. Frank Walker; 1916)

BAND STAND AND VAUDEVILLE STAND, HAMPTON BEACH, N. H.

HAMPTON BEACH, NEW HAMPSHIRE. Exeter, Hampton & Amesbury Street Railway Co. The Casino at Hampton Beach was owned by this 22-mile line. (Whiteborder card printed in the U.S. for Dudley & White, Hampton Beach; ca. 1920)

Main Street in Winter, KEENE, N. H.

KEENE, NEW HAMPSHIRE. Keene Electric Railway Co. The ten-mile line ran to Marlboro and Swanzey. The scene includes two trolleys, a horse-drawn sleigh, a steam railroad locomotive, several wagons and an auto. (Printed in Germany for the Keynart Co., Keene; postmarked Aug. 27, 1909)

ROCHESTER, NEW HAMPSHIRE. Dover, Somersworth & Rochester Street Railway Co. Pictured is one end of the line with its "Electric Car Waiting Station." (Printed in the U.S. for the Leighton & Valentine Co., N.Y.; postmark unclear)

UNCANOONUC MOUNTAIN, NEW HAMPSHIRE. Boston & Northern Street Railway Co., Boston, Mass. At the base of the mountain these excursionists would transfer to the incline railway to the top. To reach the base they had to ride on trackage of the Manchester, and the Manchester & Nashua, Street Railways. (Printed in Germany and published by the John B. Varick Co., Manchester, N.H., for the Uncanoonuc Incline Railway Co.; ca. 1910)

ATLANTIC CITY, NEW JERSEY. Camden & Atlantic Rail Road. The line ran along Atlantic Ave. to the ferry at Longport. It became the Atlantic City & Ocean City Rail Road Co. before being leased to the Atlantic City & Shore Rail Road Co. The double-truck open-bench car has a Bombay-type roof. (Postmarked Aug. 1, 1910)

CAMPBELL'S JUNCTION, NEW JERSEY. Jersey Central Traction Co., Keyport. At this junction the trolley from Highland Beach met the car from Red Bank. (Printed in the U.S. for the Union News Co., N.Y.; n.d.)

51

JERSEY CITY, NEW JERSEY. Public Service Railway Co., Newark. The trolley is emerging from the terminal where one transferred to the ferry to New York. The company was a consolidation of numerous lines, running as far south as Trenton and Camden. (White-border card printed in the U.S. after 1914)

JERSEY CITY, NEW JERSEY. Public Service Railway Co. Passing over houses, factories and everything else on the way to Hoboken, this car made a speedy and spectacular trip. (Printed in the U.S. for the John C. Voigt Post Card Co., Jersey City; postmarked July 31, 1909)

Trolley Service to Atlantic City,
8th Street Terminal, Ocean City, N. J.

OCEAN CITY, NEW JERSEY. Atlantic City & Shore Rail Road ''Shore Fast Line.''
One trip to Atlantic City was 30 miles, partly by third rail and partly by overhead
wire. A car left every half hour. A ride on another line, running to Longport,
involved two cars and a ferry. (Printed in the U.S.; n.d.)

ALBUQUERQUE, NEW MEXICO   Railroad Ave., looking East.

ALBUQUERQUE, NEW MEXICO. Albuquerque Traction Co. This and the Las Vegas
Transit Co. were the only two trolley lines in New Mexico. The Albuquerque line,
which ran seven miles, lasted until the beginning of 1928. (''Peacock'' card printed
in Germany for O. A. Matson Co., Albuquerque; postmarked Oct. 12, 1907)

53

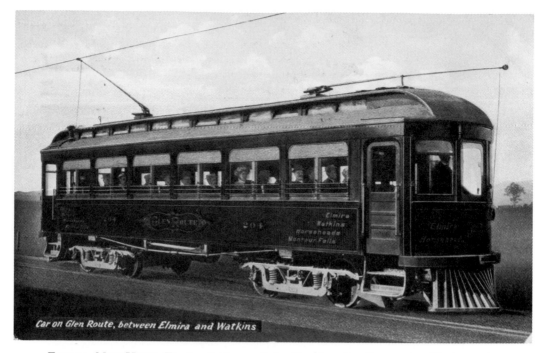

Car on Glen Route, between Elmira and Watkins

ELMIRA, NEW YORK. Elmira & Seneca Lake Traction Co. Connecting Elmira with Watkins Glen, about 20 miles away, this line was absorbed by the Elmira Water, Light & Rail Road Co. in 1916. (Printed in the U.S. for Baker Bros., Elmira; postmarked Oct. 15, 1910)

D.L.&W. Station, Fulton, N.Y.

FULTON, NEW YORK. Fulton Horse Railroad Co. This little car took passengers from the railroad to the hotels on Main St., Fulton. (Printed in the U.S.; postmarked Oct. 24, 1907)

The Patchogue-Holtsville Trolley at Holtsville, L. I.

HOLTSVILLE, NEW YORK. Suffolk Traction Co., Patchogue. This Long Island storage-battery line, with less than 12 miles of track, serviced Sayville, Bayport, Blue Point, Patchogue and Holtsville. Never electrified, its four cars operated between 1911 and 1919. The Holtsville railroad station is in the background. (Printed in the U.S.; postmarked Oct. 16, 1915)

DOUBLE DECKER, JAMESTOWN TO CELERON, CHAUTAUQUA LAKE, N.Y.

JAMESTOWN, NEW YORK. Chautauqua Traction Co. The 26-mile line serviced several towns between Chautauqua Lake (where it owned Sylvan Park) and Lake Erie. The car shown, the *Columbia,* an unusual double-decker operated by a motor-man on the upper deck, was the only one of its kind among the line's 19. There were others like it in Syracuse and elsewhere. (''Ham(m)'' postcard published by Harry H. Hamm, Erie, Pa.; n.d.)

NEW YORK, NEW YORK. Third Avenue Railway System. Generally, the elevated tracks of the Second and Third Ave. lines were over the center of the street, but not on The Bowery, where they were as widely separated as possible. (Printed in Germany for H. Hagemeister, N.Y.; photo by Brown Bros., N.Y.; postmarked May 5, 1907)

NEW YORK, NEW YORK. Third Avenue Railway System. This is how the New York entrance to the Brooklyn Bridge looked. The elevated at the left was one of the two downtown terminuses of the I.R.T. Second and Third Ave. lines. The big shed in the background was the terminus for most of the Brooklyn Rapid Transit els and for about 20 Brooklyn trolley lines. (Printed in Germany; n.d.)

New Double Deck Electric Car, New York.

NEW YORK, NEW YORK. New York Railways Co. This was the city's best-remembered double-decker, nicknamed "the Broadway Battleship." Slow and inefficient, it had only one set of "hobble-skirt" doors in the center, where the conductor sat, and stairs at the two ends. (Printed in the U.S. for the Success Postal Card Co., N.Y.; n.d.)

Monorail vs. Horse Car, City Island, N. Y.

NEW YORK, NEW YORK (Borough of The Bronx). Bronx Horse Car Line. The people in the picture are transferring from a horsecar to a monorail. Both horsecar and monorail were succeeded by the Pelham Park & City Island Railway. Ultimately the Third Ave. Railway System controlled all streetcar lines in Bronx County. ("Newvochrome" card printed in Germany for Eva Miller, City Island, N.Y.; n.d.)

NEW YORK, NEW YORK (Borough of Brooklyn). Brooklyn Rapid Transit Co. The ladies wear the "hobble skirts" that necessitated the low trolley doors and gave this make of car its nickname. The two els shown (run by the colossal company that ran the trolleys, and Brooklyn subways as well, with a total of 4292 passenger cars) are the Fulton St. el (higher level) and the Culver-Fifth Ave. line. (White-border card of the American Art Publishing Co., dated 1915; postmark unclear)

NEW YORK, NEW YORK (Borough of Queens). Brooklyn, Queens County & Suburban Railroad Co. Shown is the intersection of Jamaica and Myrtle Aves. in the Richmond Hill area before the el was built on Jamaica Ave. in 1911. (Printed in Germany; n.d.)

NEW YORK, NEW YORK (Borough of Richmond). City of New York Department of Plant & Structures. These very early trackless trolleys, with two poles and hard rubber tires, operated in one of the more remote sections of Staten Island. (Printed by the Albertype Co., Brooklyn, for W. J. Grimshaw; n.d.)

ROCHESTER, NEW YORK. Ontario Light & Traction Co. This line later became part of the New York State Railways. By 1922 it had 384 passenger cars and 104 motorized service cars on 254 miles of track. This photo was taken on Memorial Day, May 30, 1913. (Postmarked Mar. 29, 1914)

"Electricity versus Steam".

Showing the tracks of the Rochester and Eastern Rapid Railroad and the Auburn branch of the New York Central and Hudson River Railroad where they parallel each other between Rochester and Canandaigua, with the trains of each road running at full speed in the same direction. The electric car here shown is capable of making a speed of sixty miles an hour.

(VICINITY OF) ROCHESTER, NEW YORK. Rochester & Eastern Rapid Railroad. If a line by this name ever existed, it was surely absorbed into the New York State Railways conglomerate. Since the card predates 1907, the 60-mph speed of the trolley is impressive. (Printed in Germany for the Rochester News Co., Rochester; n.d.)

Centre Ave. Trolley Station, Rockville Centre, L. I.

ROCKVILLE CENTER, NEW YORK. New York & Long Island Traction Co., Hempstead. This, the leading trolley line of Nassau County, went from Jamaica via Valley Stream and Hempstead to Mineola, where it met another line of the same company that came out from Jamaica on the Jericho Turnpike. (Printed in Germany for the Montauk Cigar & Stationery Store, Rockville Center; postmarked Aug. 13, 1914)

SEA CLIFF, NEW YORK. Nassau County Railway Co. This 1.6-mile, three pantograph-car line, owned by the Long Island Rail Road, connected the Sea Cliff train station with Prospect Ave. in town. It ran from 1902 to 1924. ("Americhrome" card printed in the U.S. for Jos. E. Britt, Sea Cliff; n.d.)

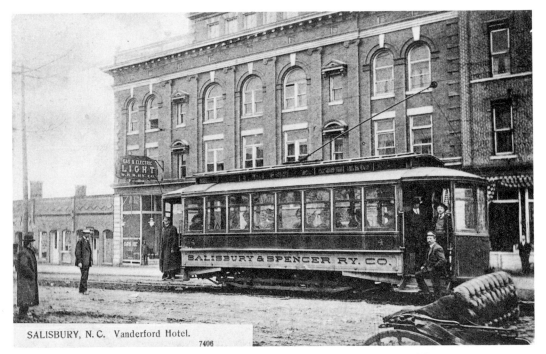

SALISBURY, NORTH CAROLINA. Salisbury & Spencer Railway Co. The company, later taken over by the North Carolina Public Service Co., ran trolleys between the two cities named, and supplied gas and electric light as well. ("Peacock" card printed in Germany; postmarked Mar. 12, 1908)

FARGO, NORTH DAKOTA. Fargo & Moorhead Street Railway Co. An interstate line with 15 miles of track and 47 cars, it connected Fargo with Moorhead, Minn., across the Red River. (Printed in the U.S. for Bloom Bros., Minneapolis; postmarked Jan. 13, 1912)

VALLEY CITY, NORTH DAKOTA. Valley City Street & Inter-Urban Railway Co. Connecting Valley City with the Soo Railroad station in North Valley City 1.5 miles away, this line handled freight and ran three passenger cars. (Published by Tom Jones, Cincinnati; probably printed in the U.S. before 1907)

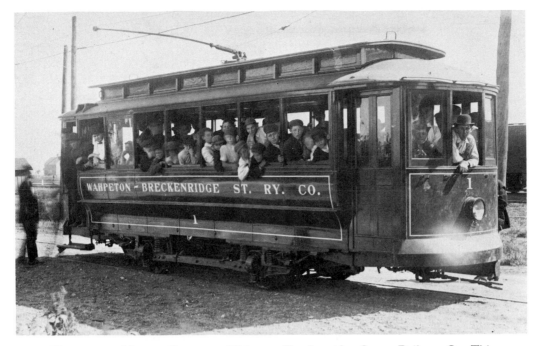

WAHPETON, NORTH DAKOTA. Wahpeton-Breckenridge Street Railway Co. This 1.5-mile, two-car line connected Wahpeton with Breckenridge, Minn. (Original-photograph card; n.d.)

CINCINNATI, OHIO. Mount Adams & Eden Park Inclined [*sic*] Railway Co. This line, part of the Cincinnati Street Railway Co. after 1896, carried its passengers right up and down the Mount Adams funicular in the trolleys themselves. (Printed in Germany for the Kraemer Art Co., Cincinnati; postmark illegible)

CINCINNATI, OHIO. Line unknown. The "Old Old Dummy" obviously ran by steam although there is also visual evidence that the line was electrified. It was probably no longer in operation when the card was mailed. (Printed in Germany for the Kraemer Art Co., Cincinnati; postmarked Apr. 7, 1909)

Euclid Ave. & 55th St. Looking East, Cleveland, Ohio

CLEVELAND, OHIO. Cleveland Electric Railway Co. This open trolley was bound for Euclid Beach. Ohio was the first, and probably only, state whose legislature subsequently prohibited the use of such open-bench summer cars. ("Litho-Chrome" card printed in Germany for the Cleveland News Co., Cleveland; postmarked Sept. 1, 1908)

LISBON, OHIO. Youngstown & Ohio River Railroad Co., Leetonia. Servicing Salem, Washingtonville and Leetonia, this 38-mile line never went near Youngstown but connected with another company that did. (Printed in the U.S. for the Bagley Co., East Liverpool; n.d.)

NELSONVILLE, OHIO. Hocking & Sunday Creek Traction Co. This is a McKeen car like the one shown in the San Diego, California view. This line, which did a lot of freight business, was electrified by 1918, when it had 15¼ miles of track. (Printed in the U.S.; mailed as a souvenir in 1947)

TOLEDO, OHIO. Toledo Traction Co. Summit St. is decorated for the National Convention of the Grand Army of the Republic. The little single-truck trolley, with its oversized railroad-type roof, is bound for Walbridge Park. (Original-photograph card; postmarked Sept. 15, 1908)

SAND SPRINGS, OKLAHOMA. Sand Springs Railway Co., Tulsa. The near trolley in the picture is not an open car but one of the longest convertibles ever built, the platforms at the two ends serving as entrances and observation areas. The car in the background is a McKeen. The 30-mile line ran between Tulsa and Sand Springs, where the company controlled the park. (Probably printed in Germany; published by the Tulsa Indian Trading Co.; n.d.)

Main Street, Tulsa, I. T.

TULSA, OKLAHOMA. Tulsa Traction Co. Oklahoma was still Indian Territory at the time of this card, but Tulsa already had three different trolley lines. (Printed in Germany; postmarked Mar. 23, 1908)

COMMERCIAL STREET, ASTORIA, OREGON.

ASTORIA, OREGON. Pacific Power & Light Co. This company also controlled the Walla Walla Valley Railway Co. in Washington. The Astoria operation had 5.5 miles of track and 26 cars of all kinds in 1918. (Printed in Germany; imported by C. E. Wheelock & Co., Peoria, Ill.; published locally by Sprouse & Son, Tacoma, Wash.; n.d.)

KLAMATH FALLS, OREGON. Klamath Falls Land & Transportation Co. Known as the "Linkville Trolley," this horsecar line was never electrified. It operated only between 1907 and 1910, connecting the Southern Pacific depot with the boat dock. (Original-photograph card published by the Miller Photo Co., Klamath Falls; postmark unclear)

PORTLAND, OREGON. Portland Railway, Light & Power Co. By 1906 this company had taken over practically every streetcar line in Portland, including this colorful observation car. It had a total of 305 miles of track and 579 electric passenger cars. (Printed by the Simplicity Co., Grand Rapids, Mich. for the Peterson & Alton Advertising Co., Portland; n.d.)

DU BOIS, PENNSYLVANIA. Du Bois Electric & Traction Co. (or Du Bois Traction Co., or United Traction Street Railway Co.). This single-truck, six-bench open car met the trains at the Buffalo, Rochester & Pittsburgh Railroad station. (White-border card printed in the U.S. for I. Robbins & Son, Pittsburgh; after 1914)

P.H.B. and N.R.R., Ellwood City, Pa.

ELLWOOD CITY, PENNSYLVANIA. Pittsburgh, Harmony, Butler & Newcastle [sic] Railway Co., Pittsburgh. This "Harmony Route," which served many towns north of Pittsburgh, was represented on some of the most beautiful trolley postcards in America. The car in the picture is off its tracks. (Printed in Great Britain for the Valentine & Sons Publishing Co., N.Y.; postmarked Mar. 22, 1910)

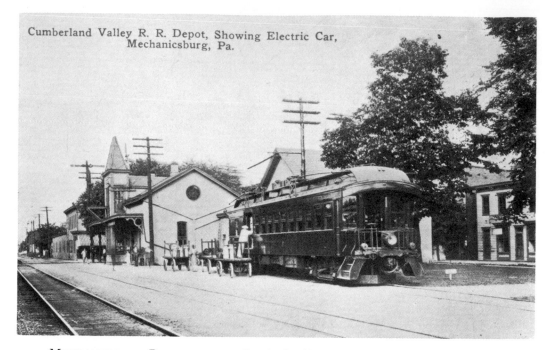

MECHANICSBURG, PENNSYLVANIA. Cumberland Valley Railroad Co. Between 1905 and 1928 this railroad electrified the branch between Dillsburg and Mechanicsburg. An unusual feature of the open-platform passenger coach was its four trolley poles, two at each end; the trolley wire was off to one side of the track in order not to interfere with the steam trains. (Published by W. A. Huber, Mechanicsburg; n.d.)

MOUNT GRETNA, PENNSYLVANIA. Cornwall & Lebanon Railroad. In order to supplement steam service from Lebanon to Mount Gretna—which early in this century was a park, camp-meeting ground and summer military camp—the railroad used this gasoline car for many years. The company later sold out to the Pennsylvania Railroad. (Printed by G. V. Millar & Co., Scranton, Pa. for Dissinger & Lesher; postmarked July 12, 1911)

PHILADELPHIA, PENNSYLVANIA. Philadelphia Rapid Transit Co. At the foot of Market St., where the ferry to Camden, N. J. was located, occurred this hard-to-negotiate trolley loop. (Postmarked Oct. 16, 1911)

PITTSBURGH, PENNSYLVANIA. Pittsburgh Railways Co. Pittsburgh, still one of the best trolley centers left in America, had already experimented with a double-decker (the first in the country) about 1890. Later it had six big closed double-deckers like the one on the card. They proved difficult to load and unload, and the trolley poles were constantly coming off the wires. (White-border card printed in the U.S. for the H. A. Schafer News Co., Pittsburgh; postmarked July 9, 1924)

71

WILLIAMSTOWN, PENNSYLVANIA. Lykens & Williams Valley Street Railway Co. This weird crossing was forced on the trolley company by the railroad line in the name of safety. The Lykens line ran only ten miles and had only ten cars. The "D & S" printed on the card is a mystery. (Printed by G. V. Millar & Co., Scranton, Pa.; postmark unclear)

YORK, PENNSYLVANIA. York Railways Co. Various types of trolleys are represented at this Center Square meet for exchanging passengers. The line had 85 miles of track and 70 motorized passenger cars. (Printed in Germany; n.d.)

SAN JUAN, PUERTO RICO. Porto Rico Railway, Light & Power Co. The three trolleys lined up next to the Post Office appear to be convertibles. The operation was electrified for 14½ miles, steam for another 18. (Original-photograph card; postmarked Feb. 18, 1924)

BLOCK ISLAND, RHODE ISLAND. Block Island Horse Car Co. This line, which was never electrified, was one of the most elaborate horse railroads in America, covering all island needs. (Printed in Germany for the Hugh C. Leighton Co., Portland, Me.; n.d.)

PROVIDENCE, RHODE ISLAND. Union Railroad Co. In the background, to the right of the Board of Trade Building, is the cable car ascending College Hill. All these trolleys later became part of the Rhode Island Co. (''Mezzochrome'' card printed in Germany for the Rhode Island News Co., Providence; n.d.)

PROVIDENCE, RHODE ISLAND. Rhode Island Co. This big conglomerate owned all the trolley lines in Providence, Pawtucket and Woonsocket, and also had trackage in Connecticut and Massachusetts. It reached several amusement parks, including Crescent Park. The last trolleys in Providence ran in 1948. (Printed in Germany for the Robbins Bros. Co., Boston; postmarked Jan. 19, 1909)

CHARLESTON, SOUTH CAROLINA. Charleston Consolidated Railway, Gas & Electric Co. This local line connected the city with North Charleston, the U.S. Navy Yard and outlying parks. Another connecting line ran nine miles to the Isle of Palms. (Printed in England for the Valentine & Sons Publishing Co., N.Y.; n.d.)

ABERDEEN, SOUTH DAKOTA. Aberdeen Railway Co. With 5.85 miles of track and ten passenger cars in 1918, this line connected Aberdeen and its suburbs between 1910 and 1922. (Postmarked Apr. 27, 1913)

The Three Tracks, Lead, S. D.

LEAD, SOUTH DAKOTA. Chicago, Burlington & Quincy Railroad. This four-mile line was operated by the railroad that serviced the area. Mining cars are running on the top level seen in the picture, a passenger railroad train in the center, and the electric trolley below. (Printed in Leipzig, Germany for Bloom Bros., Minneapolis; n.d.)

PAULTON BLOCK, SIOUX FALLS, S. D.

SIOUX FALLS, SOUTH DAKOTA. Sioux Falls Traction System. Chartered in 1907, this 16-car line ran to a few other towns on a total of 15 miles of track. (No place, no date)

MEMPHIS, TENNESSEE. Memphis Street Railway Co. This line had 124 miles of track and 344 motorized passenger cars in 1918. (White-border card printed in the U.S. for Memphis Paper Co., Memphis; ca. 1920)

AMARILLO, TEXAS. Amarillo Street Railway Co. These little four-wheel wooden box cars rambled through the streets of the Panhandle's leading city until 1920. The city then took over the line from 1920 to 1923, when it was finally abandoned. (Printed in the U.S. for H. G. Zimmerman & Co., Chicago; n.d.)

PORT ARTHUR, TEXAS. Port Arthur Traction Co. Perhaps the weirdest trolleys ever built, these were called Barber cars (made by the Barber Car Co. of York, Pa., 1908–14) and were used in Watertown, N.Y. and Sunbury, Pa. as well. The Port Arthur line ran until 1937. (Printed in the U.S. for the W. Hada Curio Store, Port Arthur; postmarked July 22, 1912)

SAN ANTONIO, TEXAS. San Antonio Traction Co. This close-up was taken on Government Hill near Fort Sam Houston. The observation trip was 40 miles long. (Printed in Germany for Ebers-White, San Antonio; n.d.)

SEGUIN, TEXAS. Seguin Street Railway Co. This mule car roamed through Seguin before 1910. This line was never converted to electricity. (''Photochrom'' card of the C. T. Co., Chicago; n.d.)

SALT LAKE CITY, UTAH. Utah Light & Railway Co. The company, incorporated in 1904, controlled practically all the city's electric light and streetcar operations. (Printed in the U.S. for the Souvenir Novelty Co., Salt Lake City; postmarked Feb. 7, 1913)

Main Street, looking North, Barre, Vt.

214904

BARRE, VERMONT. Barre & Montpelier Traction & Power Co., Montpelier. Shown is the transfer point at the center of Barre. The ten-mile line connecting the two named towns also owned two ''electric parks,'' one of which, Dewey Park, was named for Admiral George Dewey, a native of Montpelier. (Printed in the U.S. by the Leighton & Valentine Co., N.Y.; n.d.)

BRATTLEBORO, VERMONT. Brattleboro Street Railway Co. Rudyard Kipling campaigned against the building of this line for reasons that would now be connected with disruption of the ecology. It had 5½ miles of track and four motorized cars. (''Phostint'' card of the Detroit Publishing Co.; postmarked Aug. 10, 1908)

80

Burlington, Vt., R.R. Station

BURLINGTON, VERMONT. Burlington Traction Co. The 12-mile line (1893–1929) connected Burlington with Essex Junction and Winooski; an affiliated line ran to Fort Ethan Allen. (Printed in Germany for the Hugh C. Leighton Co., Portland, Me.; postmarked July 5, 1909)

The First Electric Car into Fair Haven, Vt.

FAIR HAVEN, VERMONT. Rutland Railway Light & Power Co. This is the town furthest west ever reached by the line. The tracks, obviously just laid (1902), have no ballast. (Printed in Germany for the United Art Publishing Co., N.Y.; postmarked Aug. 23, 1907)

NEWPORT NEWS, VIRGINIA. Newport News & Hampton Railway, Gas & Electric Co., Hampton. Later taken over by the Virginia Railway & Power Co., the line had over 47 miles of track, with 119 cars of all descriptions in 1918. (Probably printed in the U.S.; n.d.)

RADFORD, VIRGINIA. Radford Water Power Co. All three of the cars owned by this line are depicted. Connecting Radford and East Radford (in the west of the state, near the West Virginia border), it had less than three miles of track. (Printed in Germany for A. M. Simon, N.Y.; postmarked illegible)

17th Street Electric Car Station,
Virginia Beach, Va.

Copyright by H. C. Mann.

VIRGINIA BEACH, VIRGINIA. Norfolk Southern Rail Road Co. A suburban line connecting Norfolk with Virginia Beach, this had 47 miles of electrified track (out of a total of 900 for the railroad) and 25 motorized cars in 1918. (Printed in the U.S. for Louis Kaufmann & Sons, Baltimore; photo by H. C. Mann; postmarked Oct. 31, 1913)

All Aboard for the Lakes!

SPOKANE, WASHINGTON. Spokane & Inland Empire Rail Road Co. Shown is the Spokane terminal at Main and Lincoln Sts., the starting point for trains to Coeur d'Alene and Hayden Lakes and the St. Joe River (all in Idaho). In 1922 this division had 138 miles of track and 88 passenger interurban cars. (Printed in Germany; n.d.)

7037 Looking West on Ninth Street, Tacoma, Washington

TACOMA, WASHINGTON. Tacoma Railway & Power Co. This is one of eight cable-grip cars that ran 1.6 miles up Ninth St. The same company had 92 standard-gauge passenger trolleys running to the suburbs, owned Spanaway Park and leased the Tacoma Municipal Railway (''Tide Flats'' line). (Printed by Britton & Rey, San Francisco; n.d.)

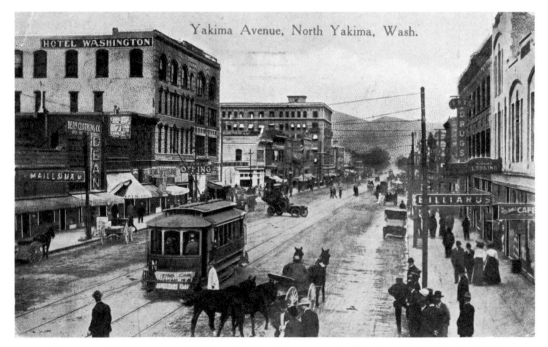

Yakima Avenue, North Yakima, Wash.

YAKIMA, WASHINGTON. Yakima Valley Transportation Co. In 1918 this line had 45 miles of track and a total of 39 cars of all kinds. Yakima is the first American city to bring back trolleys after they were gone (see color section for details). (Souvenir Post Card Co. card published by the Spokane Post Card Co., Spokane; postmarked Aug. 1, 1914)

College Viaduct, Wellsburg and Bethany Inter Urban.

WELLSBURG, WEST VIRGINIA. Wellsburg, Bethany & Washington Railway Co. Connecting Wellsburg and Bethany, this line ran 7.8 miles and had eight cars in 1918. (No place, no date)

Division Street, looking North, East Iwy, Wis.

EAST TROY, WISCONSIN. The Milwaukee Electric Railway & Light Co. This extralong, 14-window car was typical of those used in Milwaukee. The line owned over 400 miles of track and had nearly 800 cars in 1918. The "Iwy" on the card was surely meant to be "Troy." (Printed in Germany for C. H. Zinn; postmarked May 9, 1911)

Base Ball Enthusiasts, Eau Claire, Wis.

EAU CLAIRE, WISCONSIN. Wisconsin-Minnesota Light & Power Co. This company operated local lines in Eau Claire and Chippewa Falls and connected the two. It never ran trolleys to or in Minnesota, through it may have sold electric power there. (Printed by the Independent Five & Ten Cent Stores; postmarked Jan. 20, 1912)

MAVES
1896

OSHKOSH, WISCONSIN. Oshkosh Street Railway Co. By 1918 this line was electrified and, with several others, was operated by the Eastern Wisconsin Electric Co. (Original-photograph card; photo by Maves, 1896)

86

8241. Sheboygan Falls Junction.

SHEBOYGAN FALLS, WISCONSIN. Milwaukee Northern Railway Co., Cedarburg. Among the most beautiful interurbans ever built, these cars ran from Milwaukee to Sheboygan, with a transfer point at Sheboygan Falls. In 1918 there were 70 miles in operation, with 24 cars. (Probably printed in the U.S.; n.d.)

Sheridan Inn, Sheridan, Wyoming.

SHERIDAN, WYOMING. Sheridan Railway & Light Co. This line ran 16½ miles from Sheridan to Monarch. It had 12 cars. The trolley tycoon Albert Emanuel of Dayton, Ohio was one of the directors of the company, which in 1910 issued $800,000 worth of stock and $400,000 worth of bonds. (Printed in the U.S. for Herbert Coffeen, Sheridan; postmarked July 1, 1913)